Safar (The Journey)

Written By
Juveriya Azmathulla

WHAT IS PRIUN?

P: Publishing

R: Roof

I: Incredible verse

U: Utmost

N: Navigable

Priun Publication is not only publication house but an idea to giveplatform to the authors who spent a lot of efforts on their content but does not get much royalty out of their books.

Priun Publication founder Priyanka Sharma has a unique idea to set up thepublication house with the help of people who were already in the fieldand have an idea to put the authors to their readers in a unique way.Readers always look for the flavour set to their mood and we ensure the reader get its flavour from us. This Publication house is dedicated to all such talents who want to put their talent to the readers directly from heart and be the rightful owner of their book. We have taken an oath to manage every author's expectation.

ISBN: - 978-93-90994-40-3

Editor: -Juveriya Azmathulla

Disclaimer

The work in this book is entirely in the form of Fiction. The content given by the author is purely their work and is not plagiarized. It reflects the author's present recollections of experiences over time. We have tried our best to delete the plagiarized content and show the original works of the Author. The write-ups of the author contributing towards the book are unpublished. Yet, if there is something that we have missed out and any discrepancy is found, then we shall not be deemed liable for the same.

Acknowledgment

I thank each person who has supported me throughout this project and finishing my book. I thank the project manager of the Publication. I also thank everyone who styled, printed, and designed the book.

Author

Juveriya Azmathulla

About the Author

Life changes but your motives don't! Changes are permanent but you yourself aren't. Juveriya is a 21 year old girl who is back with the second part of her anthology Seher, named as Safar – The journey! Talking about her journey, she is a graduate in Bsc Nutrition and works in the corporate world currently and aims to become a full time writer someday! She is a poetess and shares her interest in public speaking, writing in various ways, singing and engaging herself in everything that brings her peace. She is also a part of a foundation named JCI (junior chamber international). She has a deep thought process and is multi-talented. She believes in keeping herself equipped in various activities that are beneficial to her as an individual. She has won many Spell bee competitions, debates, public speaking and poetry competitions apart from the very common acting,singing, chess and dance competitions.

Some words from the Author Juveriya

Not just the first book or the second, even if I were to write numerous books in my whole lifetime they would all be dedicated to my only brother, Tousif Shareef, Always and forever! I also want to dedicate this book to my Favourite cousin, Noora Al khoori. She is indeed an inspiration to me. Talking about inspiration I would not miss dedicating it to my best friends too, who are my family. If Seher happened to be about heartbreak, Safar will be about moving on further as life is a journey and there are many good things that fall ahead of you. The combination of Urdu and English poetry remains the same in this anthology too. A new and unique factor about Safar is, it has Palindrome poetry in the english sections of the book. Palindrome poetry is very rarely written and has the same words when read from the ends. I also wanted every reader to get used to the term Palindrome poetry and the uniqueness it holds. I practised and tried to write my poetry in an effective yet simple way which is easily understandable by every reader who chooses to pick it up and go through it. And if you are here reading this and going ahead, all I would truly wanna say is, thank you from the bottom most part of my heart for connecting with my work and giving me the happiest dose of encouragement.

Happy reading!!!

Table of contents

ENGLISH POETRY

SUMMARY

Seher marks the beginning of the day, which means nothing but the morning and Safar defines the journey that falls ahead! When you begin with the day and you go ahead do infinite things throughout the day before the dawn that might resemble the title of this book! Safar – The journey is yet another part of the lovely 2 language combination poetry which is combined together to form an anthology. If the morning doesn't mark the beginning of your happiness, then find it in the journey ahead.

Urdu Poetry

1. TABDEELIYAA

Teri maujoodgi me jo alfaaz jame,
Teri judaai par wahi lafz kitaab bane.

Teri mohabbat jab dheere dheere ek sawaal bani,
Tootkar wo likhi gayi har shayar kitni kamaal bani.

Tu jis din mujhe chordkar jaa raha tha,
Ek behtar raasta mujhe dusri taraf bula raha tha.

Mujhe kaha gaya tha mai uski dusri mohabbat hu shayad se,
Bada afsos hua jab jaana usne ishq seekha kisi galat riwayat se!

Meaning:

Maujoodgi = Presence

Behtar = Better

Riwaayat = tradition

2. SUKOON

Raaste me wo chord jaaye toh manzil badallo,
Inteqaam ki aag me jalna toh buzdilo ka kaam hai!

Gumshuda mohabbat me log jaan ke sadqe kyu waare,
Aakhirkaar ek din hona tujhe uske dil aur sheher me gumnaam hai!

Ansuo se saare ashiqo ke ek jazbaat banakar likhdu kya?
Har dard ko jodkar ek shayari banade yahi toh ek shayara ka kaam hai!

Aj ishq me mubtila kal usi ki nafrat ka shikaar hai,
Khel kood ki umr me ye zamane me jismi mohabbat kitni aam hai!

Saari umr baaki guzaarne ko abhi se hamsafar dhundna jayaz hai kya?
Mere dil me bina mohabbat aur jhoote sachhe waado ke bina dekho kitna araam hai!

Meaning:

Buzdil = coward

Gumshuda = lost

Shayara = poetess

Mubtila = involved

3. EK ANMOL SAHARA

Kabhi khushmizaaji ke talluq se ham bhi jaane jaate the,
Kabhi ham bhi zindagi ke ghamgheen waqto me khushi ke taraane gaate the!

Mai mohabbat ko kareeb se dekhna chahti thi,
Wo har lamha har waqt mere bazu the!

Ek daur tha isi masroof zindagi me,
Jab mere bhaiya mujhe har taane pe bila wajah hasate the.

Mai likhkar bhi lafzo me jaan na phook saki,
Wo ek muskaan se mujhe mere zindagi ke maksad ki yaad dilate the!

Mai khushiyo ko apne hi hatho se door bhejti thi aur wo wapas se kheench ke laate the!
Kabhi sabr ke mudde se ham hargiz waqif nahi hona chahte the,

Kabhi ham bhi apne zindagi se mutmayin the phir bhi khaamiyaa batate the!

MEANING:

Khushmizaaji = Jolly nature
Khaamiyaa = Flaws
Mutmayin = content

4. RIWAYAT-E- ISHQ

Mohabbat ko samajhkar chordena aur mohabbat ko chorkar samajhna do Bar aks kinare hai
Kuch log mohabbat ki ghair maujoodgi ke, toh kuch uske maujoodgi ke sahare hai

Ha Ham mitti ke, lekin ye dil sheeshe ka bana toot kyu jata hai?
Keemti rishta itna ehem darja dene ke bawajood bhi choot kyu jata hai?

Kareebi lamho ka mohtaj nahi hai mera ishq, ye shaksiyat-shaksiyat ki baat hai,
Mudkar bina dekhe bhi ishq ke huqooq ada karjaye ye tarbiyat-tarbiyat ki baat hai!

Ek martaba toota hua dil dobara mitti ka ban jata hai shayad se,
Ishq ki sakhtiyo ke baad khushi khushi samjhote banaleta hai suna hai kisi riwayat se!

Meaning:

Shakhsiyat = personality

Tarbiyat = Upbringing

Maujoodgi = presence

5. HUSN-E-AAMAAL

Lazzat hi nahi rahi ishq ke pakwaan me,
Kyuki mazbooti baaki nahi rahi ashiqo ke armaan me!

Wo ishq karte karte galtiyo ki ginti na rakhta tha,
Mere ishq me hokar dusro ki kashish ka maza chakta tha.

Ilzamo ki parchi mere naam ki kaati jaarahi hai,
Burai ki tasveer mere naam se baati jaarahi hai.

Wo karle jo uski manmaani lekin waqt aisa bhi toh ayega
Uske hotho pe mere chakhe hue pyar ka maza rehjayega

Wo dhoondega mohabbat aur sukoon kisi shaks me,
Lekin paayega meri bhoori bhoori aankhe chupi uski aks me!

Meaning:

Ilzam = Blame

Lazzat = taste

Kashish = attraction

Ginti = count

6. KHWAAB

Mai haasil karna chahu lekin paa na saku,
Mai mohabbat beintehaa karti hu lekin bata na saku.

Mai lafzo ke daayre bana chuki hu,
Mai tujhe dil me bas ek khwaab sa saja chuki hu!

Mai kadam kadam par zindagi ke faislo par aitbaar karna seekh rahi hu,
Mai bina maqsad ke bhi tum par beintehaa marna seekh rahi hu!

Mai bewafai ke baad bhi mohabbat nibha chuki hu,
Maine bataya na tujhe dil me khwaab sa saja chuki hu.

Meaning:

Haasil = acclaim

Beintehaa = limitless

Maqsad = motive

Saja = decorate

Daayre = boundaries

7. ISHQ – Ek shakhsiyat

Shayar toh the lekin hamare mohabbat ke lafzo me jaan na thi,
Hamari aur ishq ki itni kareebi koi jaan pehchaan na thi.

Jazbaato ki nadiyo me se sabse gehri nadi mohabbat wali thi,
Aur ham uss leher ke kareeb tehre the jo sabse shiddat wali thi.

Iss nadi me doob kar hum kinare ki talash me the,
Kismat ki lakeero ko modkar hum sahare ki talash me the.

Kuch gehri mohabbat karne walo ka apna alag muqaam hai,
Ye himmat,aitebaar ki baat hai ya kismat ka Intezaam hai.

Meaning:

Pehchaan = identity

Leher = wave

Aitebaar = trust

Muqaam = position

8. BEKHABAR

Ishq me haar jeet ki baat karna na munasib hai,
Lekin shayad se haarkar hi ishq ko samajhna wajib hai!

Mujhe ishq me sa se judi shiddat kya hai bata dena,
Jisne mujhse pehli nazar me ishq kiya zara uska pata dena!

Mere nazro ke saamne, par mujhse aankh nahi mila paata,
Iss nasl me shayad abhi tak aisa pyar kiya nahi jaata?

Mai jab jab muskati hu toh ankho ke kinaro se dikhti hai uski hasi,
Mere tukde se wajood me kisi ki saari umeede iss tarah kaise basi?

Mujhe samajh nahi aa raha tha ki maine mohabbat kyu nahi ki,
Ab samajh araha hai ki kisi ke ishq ke kitaab ka har panna mai hi thi!

Kisi ne ishq se talluq se bas mera hi naam joda,
Kisi ka dil barso se aj talak hamne kyu berukhi se toda?

Meaning:
Shiddat = Passion
Berukhi = Ruthlessly
Munasib = appropriate
Muskati = to smile

9.AASHIQ MIZAAJ (Casanova)

Tabah tabah hui ek dafa ishq ka toofaan aaya tha,
Hamko na pata bas kuch pal basne ke liye dil me mehman aaya tha!

Rooh se ham alfaaz pesh karte aur unka purana karobaar tha,
Phir bhi kambhakht ishq unki raaho me fanah hone ke liye tayyar tha

Unki zubaan pe kayi naam aur har naam se mohabbat beintehaa aisa jatate the,
Wo har dusre din akele me nayi nayi mohabbato ko jhooti mohabbat ki raah dikhate the

Mai haske chaar baate aj bhi karleti hu beshak se,
Lekin samajh nahi aata wo raabta toh karte hai lekin kiss haq se?

Uska dil ishq se hara bhara aur mujhme bhi wo jazbaat jagaye the,
Usne mohabbat ke naam pe na jaane dil me kitne kamre banaye the!

Meaning:
Mehmaan = guests
Raah = way
Beshak = undoubtedly
Tabah = Ruined
Karobaar = Business

10.KUCH EHEM SAWAL

Chaand taare todna na mumkin hai,
Tum chand phool todke laa doge kya?
Apna dil mujhe bhale mat dena,
Lekin mera toota hua dil jodke laa doge kya?
Ansoo chahe na lo mere,
Bas khushiyo ki hawa ko meri taraf modke laa doge kya?
Maazi chahe jaisa b ho,
Apne aaj aur kal ka mujhe ek ehem hissa bana loge kya?
Mehenge tohfe aur khwahishat na sahi,
Mujhe bas jayaz waqt deke har baat pe mana loge kya?
Jhoote waade sabhi karte hai,
Lekin tum sach me zindagi bhar sath nibha loge kya?

Meaning:

Mehenge = costly

Maazi = past

11.MOHABBAT AUR MUSTAKBIL

Tahammul aur tahaffuz mohabbat se jude hue hai ye tumse hi toh milkar jaana
Ek taraf tumhare liye dil me mohabbat aur dusri taraf ye sara zamana!

Aamal aur lafz se hi nahi ham toh khayalo me bhi tumhe takleef dene ka nahi sochte,
Har ishq ki kitaab ka panna padhte padhte ham bas tumhe hi kyu khojte?

Andaaza toh bilkul nahi tha lekin Tadbir bhi tu taqdir bhi tu,
Dil me mohabbat ke naam par banjaye wo ek lauthi tasveer bhi tu!

Maazi se bhi raazi hu, mohabbat toh mustaqbil ki ek dor hai,
Saari duniya meri sooni sooni si, bas dil me tere ishq ka shor hai!

Meaning:

Tahammul = patience

Tahaffuz = protection

Tadbir = Planning

Taqdir = Destiny

12.ISTEHKAM

Agar kisi ki talab aur uska nasha itna sukoon deh ho sakta hai,
Toh mujh jaisa insan uske hi pyar me mubtila ho sakta hai.

Mai chahe jitna bhi chupalu uski mohabbat ko apne dil ke ghere me,
Uske zikr par mere ankho ki chamak jaisa izhar kya ho sakta hai?

Nafrat har kisi se kar baithe kyuki lagne laga har koi rakeeb ho sakta hai,
Meelo door lekin kabhi socha na tha phir bhi koi dil ke itna kareeb ho sakta hai,

Kuch is tarah apne nigaho ka jaam pilaya h apne,
Is shamma ko apna parwana banaya h apne

Har lamha khayalo ke darwaze par dastak de jate ho,
Isi tarah toh door rehkar b Nazdeekiyo ko badhaya hai apne

Rooh se mohabbat bhi kar hi lege
Roooh see mohabbat bhii kar hi lege
Filhal toh dil ke rom rom ko mohabbat ke purzo se sajaya hai apne!

Meaning:
Purza = part
Chamak = shine
Nigah = Sight
Dastak = To knock

13.EK NAYI SHAKHSIYAT

Ab nahi hoti baate, mushk si raate karne!
Ab nahi tarasta dil, ishq ki baate karne.

Tawajjuh na diya tha aamaalo pe apne ashiq ke,
Tawajjuh na diya tha aamaalo pe apne ashiq ke,

Nikal pade the mohabbat ke naam ki zakaate karne,
Lekin ab nahi tarasta dil, ishq ki baate karne.

Kaisi aapasdaari nibhane pe majboor horahe hai,
Kaisi, aapasdaari nibhane pe majboor horahe hai,

Dil tootne par kadam badh rahe hai rishte naate karne,
Isiliye ab nahi tarasta dil ishq ki baate karne

Ehmiyat chahe saari lutado, lekin izzat mehfooz nahi
hoti,
Mohabbat ke badle intezaar aur badlehaazi mil rahi hoti.

Wapasi ke raaste dekhkar aana meri gali me ishq ki
barsaate karne,
Kyuki ab mera dil nahi tarasta ishq ki baate karne.

Meaning:

Amaal = deeds
Aapasdaari = companionship
Tawajjuh= attention

14.AAM SA DHOKA

Ishq me tahaffuz hai, aisa bayaan kiya jata hai,
Alfazo me zeher gholkar naya anjaam diya jata hai.

Bikhre hue tukde dil ke sametne me waqt lag jaata hai,
Usi shaqs ke hatho, tahaffuz
Wapas mang liya jata hai!

Talq baato se dil ke aar paar nafrat bikherdo,
Gum dil ke andhero me wahi mohabbat ka armaan jiya jata hai

Dil ke aetraaf mohabbat ko gherkar dekha,
Beintehaa mohabbat lutakar ek dafa mu pherkar dekha.

Tajweed sikha rahe the ham usko zindagi ki,
Har harkaat chod usne mujhe niche zer kar dekha!

Takalluf mat karna nafrat lutane ki us shakhsiyat pe,
Banjar dil ki zameen me ek waqt par usne mohabbat ke beenj ko per kar dekha.

Meaning:

Zeher = poison
Mu pherna = to turn heads
Aetraaf = surrounded by
Sametne = to gather

15.CHOOTA

Meri zindagi ka maksad pucha gaya, mai haske, tere baare sochne laga,
Ek dafa Tu har lamha mere paas tha phir achanak Mai apni neend se jaga!

Mai kon hu jo mohabbat par waqt ki pabandiya lagadu,
Mohabbat toh mohabbat hai, lekin isko kaise apne dil me jagah du?

Maine mehfooz tariqo se apni mohabbat ko sambhalna chaha par wo hua nahi,
Sabke gale lag rahi thi mohabbat aur mujhko ghaafil ne dekho chua nahi.

Maine jazbaat bikhere, dard chaap diya, logo ne use shaayari batadiya,
Ham shauqeen ne bhi phir mohabbat se mohabbat ko apne kalam se sajadiya.

Meaning:

Tariqe = techniques

Chaap = print

Pabandiya = restrictions

16.SABKH-E- MOHABBAT

Kisi se bepanah pyar karna na mumkin nahi hota,
Kuch rishto ko alfazo me bayaan karna mumkin nahi hota.

Ek zamane se zindagi ke safar ka mustaqil hissa ho tum,
Zindagi ke har panne pe likha hua lazim sa ek qissa ho tum.

Ab nahi pata maksad aur maza bacha bhi hai kya jeene me?
Haal hi me ishq ne dard bhara hai mere seene me!

Tu zindagi bhar mujhko yaad rahega mere mohabbat ka ye kasoor hai,
Ham jawaan rooho ko ye dekhte dikhate dil tudwane ka kaisa chada suroor hai?

Mohabbat bhi na mili, na mila sukoon, dosti bhi na mili, na mila wo junoon,
Dil ne mujhe ek tarfa bana kar rakhdiya, dimaag ki na sun paau toh aakhirkaar ab kiski sunooo??

Meaning:

Qissa = chapter
Kasoor= blame
Aakhirkar = Lastly
Bayaan = to express through word

17.DO PAL KI MOHABBAT

Aae mere khabar rakhne wale
Aate waqt akhbaar lete ana…
Tere dil ke darr par ishqq ki baate hui toh wo darbaar lete aana!

Do pal ki khushi thi phir do pal ka gham, bichde aur mile kayi dafa ham,
Par tum saare ikathha karte hue mere khatir wo pal chaar lete aana

Mai kaandhe par sar rakhkar kuch ansoo dhalaa dungi,
Tum kuch pal ke liye apne maazi se khushiyo ka sansaar lete aana

Mujhe dhundla dhundla sa nazar aane laga hai sab kuch badi der se,

Shayad mera nazariya phisal gaya toh sath hi sath wo apna jhoota pyar lete aana!

Meaning:

Dhundla = blurry
Nazariya = point of view
Dhalaa = to shed
Ikathha = collectively
Darbaar = Entrance

18.KHOOFIYA KHAUF

Pehli nazar ka pyar nahi jab har nazar me pyar ho toh mujhe tab batana,

Mai apne mukammal ek tarfa pyar me khush hu, tum mujhe apne ek tarfa pyar se na satana!

Ye zamane se doori ikhtiyaar jo karne lagi hu, mai khudse naraz hu khuda se nahi,

Purane qisse saare zindagi ke metkar naye panne se naya aghaaz karne mai khuda toh nahi?

Mera ashiq mujhko apne hi qisse me rakeeb bana baitha mujhse mera wajood aur mera ishq juda-juda toh nahi?

Mai khud ko dhoondne kayi dafa mohabbat kar baithi, mera kirdaar mujhe dhoond raha hai kahi mai khud gumshuda toh nahi?

Meaning:

Aghaaz = start

Gumshuda = lost

Ikhtiyaar = rights

19.LAT

Mai khwabo me bhi use bulana pasand karti hu,
Jazbaato ko kagaz par utar kar mai achhe lamho ko phir dohrana pasand karti hu.

Sher o shaayari karte hue log apni mohabbat par guman kare,
Alfazo ki aisi kya ehsiyat ki wo kisi ki mohabbat ko bayaan kare

Parson jab khwab me usko gale lagaya tha,
Usne Khushi ka ankaha ehsaas dil me jagaya tha.

Uske muskurahato ke kisse roz mere dil ke mohalle mein goonjte hai,
Khwabo me hi sahi ham abhi b unse mulaqat ke bahane dhundte hai🩶..

Meaning:

Goonjna = resonate

Dohrana = to repeat

Ankaha = unsaid

20.KHARAABI

Meri mohabbat na mukammal si hai toh chordu kya?
Apne dil ke toote hue tukdo ko aur tod du kya?
Behadd mushkil hai khudki chuni hui mohabbat me sukoon dhundna,
Mai apni khwahisho ko nakaamiyaabiyo se jod dh kya?
Mujhse na mil paayi lekin phir bhi, mujhse mohabbat karne ki himmat kar baithe kayi,
Mai jaha waqt bhi na mile pur sukoon, na kavishe, uss raaste se apna raasta mod du kya?
Socha tha badal kar mohabbat karte hai iss dafa, na hoge kisi baat par khafa,
Ye mere andar jo logo ne bikhere mohabbat ke maayne unko marod du kya?
Meri mohabbat na mukammal si hai toh chod du kya?
Apne dil ke toote hue tukdo ko aur tod du kya?

Meaning:

Mukammal = complete

Behadd= limitless

Nakaamiyaabi = failure

Kavishe = efforts

21. BAAT CHEET (conversational shayari)

Ladka: Yaari dosti sukoon ke asbab hai jaano.

Ladki: Mohabbat me sirf junoon hai maano na maano.

Ladka: kuch pal me bik jaaye, mukar jaye, dosti ke aise usool nahi!

Ladki: Mohabbat bhi murjha jaye, uss mohabbat me diye gaye phool jaise nahi!

Ladka: Mohabbat chod jaaye toh dosti unhi ansuo me bheeg kar rahat dhund deti hai.

Ladki: Dosti farz hai kyuki mohabbat dekho toh, lamha lamha kitne imtihaan leti hai.

Ladka: Aur agar dosti mohabbat me tabdeel ho jaye toh uski keemat gira di jaati hai.

Ladki: Dosti, dosti hai! Dosti hi rahegi. Ye haqeeqat waqt se pehle bata di jaati hai.

Meaning:
Asbaab = elements
Imtihaan = Test
Haqeeqat = reality
A/N: Conversational shayari between 2 best friends where the boy is in love with the girl. Divided in 5 parts.

22.JAWAAB – TERI AANKHEIN

Meri mohabbat zyada gehri hai ya teri ankhein?
Meri mohabbat zyada khoobsoorat hai ya teri aankhein?

Meri yaaddasht zyada tez hai ya teri ankhein?
Mere khaab zyada mojizaana hai ya teri aankhein?

Ye mohabbat ka jaam zyada nasheela hai ya teri aankhein?
Tere hone se meri duniya zyada roshan hai ya teri aankhein?

Jhooti mohabbat ke bheed me jaise ek kone me chamak rahi thi teri aankhein,
Itne saare sawal man me jag gaye aur bas ek dafa takraayi meri aur teri aankhein!

Meaning:

Mojizaana = dreamy

Takraayi = collide

Gehri = deep

Yaddasht = memory

23.BAAT CHEET (2)

Ladka: Ghuroob se pehle ka sama suhana hai par tumse zyada nahi.

Ladki: Baat khoobsurat samajh aati hai lekin hame lagta hai tumhara koi aisa irada nahi.

Ladka: Mohabbat hamari bedaagh, wafadar, dildaar si hai, aapke tajurbe ke mutabiq koi jhoota wada nahi.

Ladki: Har koi khelta hai lekin mohabbat me koi jeet haar nahi aur hamara dil koi shatranj ka pyada nahi.

Ladka: zindagi samjho ya khel, hamne toh hamari rani maangi thi kuch badhkar ya zyada nahi!

Ladki: Maazi me kya jeena junaid, ye zindagi ka safar hai koi sheher ka raasta seedha saadha nahi.

Ladka: Afsos toh ajkal is baat ka hai meri dosti ko iqteyaari samjha, koi wada nahi.

Dil na dete toh ehtemaad ki hi umeed thi aur kuch zyada nahi.

Meaning:
Ghuroob = Sunset
Bedaagh = spotless
Shatranj = chess
Ehtemaad = respect

24.DAUR-E- FAREB

Mohabbat ka falsafa hame bhi koi sikhane aaya tha,
Mohabbat ka asal me koi wajood nahi hame bhi koi dikhane aaya tha!

Ham jisko mohabbat maan baithe, unki asal me mohabbat koi aur the,
Ham pehli seedhi par khade hue hi the, unhone sunaya unke mohabbat ke toh kayi daur the!

Jis kisi ko mohabbat maano, uss mohabbat ko mohabbat kisi aur se,
Ye saare zamane bhar ke aashiko ki kahani sunna tum bade gaur se!

Usey sachhi mohabbat sabse ho baithti hai uski ye aadat kyu nahi jaati?
Munfarid ishq ki kahaniya mujhe samajh kyu nahi aati?

Dil lagte rehte hai charo taraf aaj ispe toh kal uspe marna,
Tum shiddat ki toh baat karne ki bhi gustakhi na karna.

Talab bas uski hoti hai jisko paaya hi nahi par kho baithe,
Ye kaisa zamana hai, jisne tumhe nazro se giraya tum usi ke ho baithe?

Meaning:
Falsafa = philosophy
Maano = believe
Munfarid = Unique

25.BAAT CHEET(3)

Ladki: Itna iqteyaar tha hamara tumpe par ham bekhabar the,
Itna waqt tha baaki ishq ko janne par ham besabar the.

Chakna mana tha lekin talab bohot thi mohabbat ki,
Doosre mauke mil bhi jaaye toh jagah nahi ab shiddat ki.

Ladka: Chordkar jaane par bhi uske, kitni mohabbat se tune sath nibhaya,
Uss waqt tera tootkar kisi aur ko chahna bhi mujhe pasand aaya.

Dil kaha mehfooz mehsoos karta, maine khud se kiya har waada tod diya,
Waqt ke sitam ke baad aise aalam ka tasavvur karna chordiya!

26.DOSTI YA ISHQ?

Baagho me jaake dekha kayi phoolo ka nazara,
Dilo me jhaank kar dekha toh dikha bas mohabbat ka sahara.

Raaste ke musafir hai, andaza nahi tha dilo ke andar ke sard ka,
Gulaab ke kaanto ko chookar tajurba hua chuban ke dard ka!

Rangeen mizaaj tha hamara phir log bhi rang dkhane lage,
Bol, chaal, rehen sehen ke khud hi dhand sikhane lage.

Bahut kuch maang liya tha rab se jab aasman se gira tha ek tootta taara,
Ab mere zindagi ke sur taal ko chedta rehta hai ek bhawra aawara!

Sukoon bas dosti me hai sun chuke hai kayi dafa ab samajhne bhi lage,
Is dafa se jitne bhi meethe khaab aur khwahishaat sab dosti ke naam se hi jage!

Meaning:

Baagh = field
Tajurba = experience
Khwahishaat = wishes
Aawara = castaway

27.BAAT CHEET(4)

Ladki: Talq baate ho gayi humse isiliye aankhein nam hai kya?
Kuch dino se raabta na ho paaye hum se isi baat ka gham hai kya?

Ladka: Suna hai mohabbat ki raaho me dafn kiye gaye jazbaat bhi jagte hai,
Isliye itne nazariya ka fasla hai phir bhi ap hamko itne kaatilana lagte hai.

Ladki: Mohabbat ki mehfil mein ab ye kaisi justujoo badhne lagi hai,
Ghaor farmao toh meri mohabbat ki kashti meri khushiyon ki lehron se ladne lagi hai.

Ladka: Qadar karna hai mohabbat ki lekin ham kis kis ki qadar kare,
Ham beqadar ki bhi qadar nahi hai kahi, toh chalo ikatthe sabar kare!

28.QUDRAT

Pata tha iss mitti ki dhool se uss tehni ke phool se,
Parinde ke pankh se, samandar ke shankh se,
Paani ki gehraiyon se, aasmaan ki unchaiyo se.

Badalo se bhi ishq ho jata hai,
Hawao me bhi ishq ghul jaata hai.

Muskaano se ishq khil jaata hai,
Darakhton pe lage phoolo me bhi ishq mil jaata hai!

Lekin jab se ishq baazaaru ho gaya hai,
Duniya ki har banawati cheez par, har kisi ka dil ajata hai!

Hamare paas toh waqt tha, iqteyaar tha, samajh thi,jazbaat the,
Fursat se dohraana chahte the sachhi mohabbat ke haseen pal
lekin wo kaise halat the?

Unse hi judi yaade thi, shaamein thi, duaein thi,
Khaab the,
Kyuki wo hamari ik lauthi mohabbat aur baaki sab jod jod kar
bas mohabbat ke asbab the!

Meaning:

Parinde = creatures
Darakht = Stem
Pankh = wings
Dohraana = to repeat

29.BAAT CHEET (5)

Ladka: Angdaiya madmast wo lete rahe,
Angdaaiyaa madmast wo lete rahe,
Aur neendo ko hamari uda diya.

Khwaish thi tang galiyon se guzarne ki,
Khwaish thi tang galiyon se guzarne ki,
Rab ne uske dil ka raasta pakda diya…

Ladki: Uljhan, dikkat, tehesh ab chordo saari baate,
Khushiyo ki ummeed me ajse karz hai saari raate!

Mehfile sajti rahegi subah se shaam toh hone do,
Wapas lautna hoga yahi pe thoda sukoon toh khone do.

30.NAYI KITAB

Jab hum mile toh khushi likhdi,
Juda hue toh kami likhdi,
Uski yaad me aansuo ki nami likhdi.

Purane tasveero me khushi dekhkar nayi ummeed likhdi,
Phir naye zamaane ki ishq ki salaahiyat dekhkar asliyat likhdi,
Jitna bhi chupaalu, apne lafzo ke zariye apni niyat aur tarbiyat likhdi!

Kahaniyo ko shayari me tabdeel kar maine apni jawani likhdi,
Ek baar ishq laazim karke dekhna, maine iss jazbaat se judi shayari behisaab likhdi,
Pata hi nahi chala waqt ke chalte chalte kab ek aur kitaab likhdi.

Meaning:

Laazim = must

Ummeed = hope

Chupaalu = to hide

Wah wah… wah wah!!

ENGLISH POETRY.

(How do I aid my heart, which has been bleeding from the very start?

How do I complete my story, by holding the incomplete answer to my every query?

How do I regularly smile wide, with these wounds of my heart which I'm supposed to hide?

How do I become unsuccessful in not hurting any heart, without even wishing to throw my greed's dart?

I'm the happiest for the world and the people around,

But, the complications love me immensely so they come easily to me and surround.)

1. PALINDROME POETRY

DAY BY DAY, RAYS SUN EMITS, LIFE SHINES BRIGHTLY
BRIGHTLY SHINES LIFE, EMITS SUN RAYS DAY BY DAY!

POETRY INSPIRED SMILES WORD BY WORD,
WORD BY WORD SMILES INSPIRED POETRY!

HEAD TO TOE, CELLS AND BODY CASTED OUT LOVE,
LOVE OUTCASTED BODY AND CELLS, TOE TO HEAD

EMOTION IS WHAT? DELUSION IS LOVE,
LOVE IS DELUSION, WHAT IS EMOTION?

Note: Palindromes are read the same in both the backward and forward direction

2. MEN EMPOWERMENT

Women empowerment is being promoted,
For a woman, everyday I see different appreciations regularly quoted.

Today I am going to write about the struggles a man faces,
Because this is something that we ignore in many cases.

If only someone thinks about his struggles and sacrifices everyday.
From the second he is born,he is expected to take care of the entire family one fine day.

We differentiate their existence and make their personalities complicated,
With thousand different responsibilities on his head,
He is always presumed to act sophisticated.

A brother, A son and a husband who then becomes a father.
Tell me, this kind of selflessness from where do you gather?

The different phases of life tested him with immense hardships and pressure.
You have not been regularly told but you are a woman's life's absolute treasure!

You are the owner of the smiles of your successful
female family members,
The ratio of your sacrifices is extremely high even
though everyone rarely remembers.

To fill everyone's stomach at home everyday, Through
what all have you been?
To keep everything in your heart, never cry out and
To love, encourage and absorb all the pain unseen.

This is just a thank you note for all that you have ever
been doing!
For being the most important catalyst in a woman's life
and your worth which you have been proving.

Without you every woman is incomplete,
Because every time A woman is called the word MAN
has to repeat!

3. P IN PAIN STANDS FOR POETRY

I write through my heart and not my brain!

I write like my heart is drenched in pain.

I write like these lyrics are my definition of sane!

I write for the hearts that are like droplets of rain,

And I write to romance with the words that keep me sane!

I write cause words travel through heart's every lane,

I write because turning pain into poetry is an art that shouldn't go in vain!

I write to energise because through the means of words alone I can sustain!

4. MY BEST FRIEND

Your heart and soul, I know is pure,
During times,unworthiness knocks on my door, your smile is my favourite cure.

Many adjectives together cannot define you,
Every single line in this poem of mine is absolutely true!

We might stay far away for countable days or numerous years,
I always and forever will remember you at times happy and when my eyes shed tears.

Friendship has a deeper meaning which I understood by your means,
I will never forget your support and cooperation in every crime and in all of life's epic scenes.

With you I laugh a 100 times louder,
Subsiding issues become even wider!

You are the most favourite human, and I'm saying this since forever,
But, at times you are the dumbest of all and at times the most clever.

Whatever it may be, I'll keep nurturing our friendship's tree!
I love you for the human you are,

Cheers to a lifetime with my super special, brightly shining super star!

5.DELUSION

Into a world I enter where my life knows no pain,
A world from which my sadness can very easily drain!

Where my eyes shine as bright as a diamond,
Where I'm being positioned as high as a Raymond.

I'm that one dreamer of this nature,
Who carries a vision in her eyes of her owned world's
perfect miniature.

Where my smile reveals the condition of my heart,
Where there is nothing called destiny which can set us
apart!!

Where my mind doesn't work in a scientific way,
Where after people's elimination memories don't stay!

I'm that one dreamer of this nature,
Who carries a vision in her eyes of her owned world's
perfect miniature!!

6.A PERFECT RELATIONSHIP

Love with a true soul,
Completes you on the whole!

You are my favourite ray of sunshine,
You are the only person who is exclusively mine.

That smile of yours is indeed very sweet,
And every time you wear it, it raises my heart beat

Our endless talks and every stupid fight
The happiness that doubles, after we quickly re unite!

You, my love, are the reason for loud laugh and me being shy,
A beauty like you, is worth watching without a blink of an eye.

By adding vivid colours, you made my life flip,
Cheers to our never ending relationship !

The happiness you unfurl and the love you shower, hope you know your presence is my special super power.

Bad times come and go,
But with you by my side, together we will glow.

7.RAPE – A normalised tale.

Witnessing the depletion of humanity under the screams of women.
Every 4 hours a news of rape pops up at our televisions.
Jammu & Kashmir to Tamil Nadu the whole India lacks women safety provisions!

Sometimes it's a girl in shorts, and sometimes a girl covered in abaya
Sometimes it's a grown up woman and sometimes a toddler-two years old !
During the shiny sunny day time or at 2 AM in the night,
Any minute the rapes occur and for months and years the mystery remains unfold!

Partying at night and wearing of short dresses or wearing of burqa and limiting herself to the boundary of her home,
Every other girl gets unreasonably blamed for her appearance and gets raped in India's dome.

Can't even blame the dresses we wear,
Because these irregular rape cases in India aren't rare,
From public roads to religious places this shameful activity takes place everywhere.

Ignorance of justice is justified without a proper justification.
Youngsters are readily trying hard to find a proper solution.

But, the raising voices are minimised after some
effective candle marches and a weak resolution.

How funny is it that we are still not feeling degraded?
It's time for some moral values and human ethics to get
traded
I'm shameful today for being one amongst millions of
India's daughters,
Because rapists here live a respectful life, whereas any
other national government immediately slaughters.

Every rule under every section of the Indian law is being
ignored and why are we even glad?
After this, I don't think I can step out of the house
saying, I'll return back safe mom and dad.

And this is the plight of girls in every corner of this
country.
Sadly, Rape has become a source of income for the
journalists and just a part of commentary!

8.THE GEN-Z QUESTIONNAIRE

Will I ever fall in love again? Never, Cross my heart!!
Just after a few days I'm in love again hoping for another brand new start.

How are the modern fairy tales going to end?
Falling in love and later making him your unimportant general friend.

What do I do with these questions wiggling in my mind?
Love cannot answer any of my questions as it is completely blind!!

My purest form of love is being wasted,
Because people refuse to experience it soon after it is tasted.

Love stories of my generation begin and end very normally,
In this Gen-z generation of ours is love meant to just exist formally?

9.TOXICITY

With those permanent bruises on my heart,
Life with a visible smile on my face was no more an art.

Giving up on something was not an easy task,
And so was hiding your emotions and wearing an
invisible mask.

I'm unable to clean up my heart, from Love's pollution
and dirt,
Years from now, I can still imagine myself completely
broken and hurt.

Reasons aren't enough to break a heart so delicate,
I have built my own sentence of love now, how do I
reincarnate?

No one bothered to look inside my heart and observe that
unbearable pain,
Waves and waves of my emotions, onto the papers
unpolluted and plain,
Through a faithful pen,I regularly drain.

Wanted to heal these bruises as soon as possible,
But, just a thought of your's strikes my mind and the
situation becomes uncontrollably terrible.

10.LIFE IS A LIE

Life has become a drama where I pretend to be always fine.
Broken is me and the innocent soul of mine.

Strings melodies played in my head,
Life was Picturized as an adventure in every novel I read!

Multiple emotions running down my heart, through its different chambers,
I was gradually settling down, to taste life's various flavours.

As soon as the activation of pain and psychological distress had taken place mentally.
A sensation of hurt was experienced practically.

The one who never stepped back and believed to succeed is to firstly try,
Now, has astonishingly gotten down on her knees and concludes that, LIFE IS A LIE.

Frantically, I had forgotten to introduce myself to the general suspense,
Amid my curiosity to grow and witness peace and independence.

11.A TERRIBLE DREAM

My smile shrinked completely and I gulped the saliva in,
The expression I had on my face with an unusually sweaty skin.

That murder of crows landed on my bed from different directions,
My life had forgotten its destination so left me at its various junctions.

I swept down slowly from the bed-sheet, finding myself screaming for help,
Thousands surrounded me there yet, no one could even hear my extremely painful yelp.

Tears slipped down my cheeks and happiness instantly dried,
I got up from the deep slumber and opened my eyes fully wide.

12.A JOURNEY OF LOVE

If stars cannot be counted how can my love be measured
?
In one tiny heart of mine, immense love for you is
treasured.

While I think of you, my heart gives a smile,
While we fight it definitely stops it for a while.

You are the most beautiful journey of my life,
I don't want it to end so take it further and make me your
wife.

With every blink of an eye,
Your memories make me feel shy.

In every world I am destined to choose you,
The whole world admits that you are just too good to be
true!

It takes one message of yours to disperse my stress,
Without a single doubt, you are my permanent door of
happiness.

13.YOUR EYES

There are planets, universe, galaxies and milky ways,
Then there are your bare eyes when you just step out
under direct sun rays!

There are 7 skies, clouds, earth and incomparable nature,
Then there are dreams of you in my short, sweet and
unplanned future.

There are shooting stars, twinkling stars and one whole
damn perfect moon,
Then there are your smiles that make that same night
shine bright as an afternoon!

There are infinite lovers with different techniques of
loving their lovers in world's different parts,
Then there is me with your love in this teeny tiny heart
of mine where their love ends and mine kickstarts.

14.THE MOMENT I FELL IN LOVE

And the moment I fell in love,

I became extra cheerful, happy, and glowing,

The cool breeze that touched my skin felt so comforting,

The butterflies I didn't notice before looked so alluring,

The warmth of the sun's rays made my life so brightening,

The moon which I always unnoticed seemed so scintillating,

The tiny stars which were always hiding started sparkling,

The greenery and flowers all around started to give me a positive feeling,

And my face was always mysteriously smiling.

All these signs ultimately proved that love and my life are perfectly mingling.

15.LOVE EXPLAINED IN SEASONS

In the dark, all alone at 3 Am I always wonder,
What exactly is love ? Is it an advantage or a blunder?

Creating a new definition of love everyday.
Life has turned from blue to grey!

The clock of my mind isn't ready to stop,
And the concept of love doesn't enter my head with a tik and a tok.

On a starry night, with sky filled stars,
I think of it as something that will heal my scars.

On a rainy day, with water dripping on my body and a tear rolling down on my cheek,
I think of it as a "need", a need out of my loneliness at its peak!

On an autumn morning,
With leaves falling by,
It makes me realise it's gloriously beautiful,
And makes me involuntarily shy!

Summer gives me the thirst to find out the right answer again,
But, it teaches me through its heat and warmth how love can comfort and also make you drench in pain.

Different seasons I witness different emotions,
Gushing down inside me.
Autumn, Monsoon, Summer, all the seasons add up numberless leaves to my love's tree.

16.MY PRINCE CHARMING

An ugly girl, full of flaws,
Uncertain and hopeless.
Tired of this world,
Of love and humans.
Residing in her little bubble,
With unshared thoughts,
And feelings never confessed.

Then came her,
Prince charming,
Love of her life,
Like the knight in shining armour,
Handsome, mature, handling her with care.
Immense love bestowing everyday.
A genuine being, pure and sweet.
Defining him with words,
Will make the dictionary feel brief.

Two happy souls,
Happiest than ever!
Love in its purest form,
Showing its true colour.
Every day gets them close,
Closer and closest.
It's been some months,
And the days have been the best.
Two months? Or two years?
I'm quite sure,
It's been two decades in this lovesphere.

17.FIRST LOVE

You're still that
Beautiful dream of mine,
Which will forever be incomplete.

The most favourite
Character of mine,
Which suddenly dies.

The most favourite
Book of mine,
Whose pages I have lost.

The most pleasant evening
I've ever seen,
Whose memories I've forgotten.

The most beautiful story
I've ever read,
Whose ending remains incomplete.

But above all,
You are that love of mine,
Whose feelings I can still feel.

18.STILL SO IN LOVE

Penning down a poem,
With myriad thoughts in my mind.
When I think of you,
I get different emotions completely intertwined.
Sweet, caring, arrogant, Sometimes freakish and sometimes pleasant!
Your mere presence in my life cannot so easily be defined.

Keeping all of these aside,
I can't thank you enough for offering this life's joyful ride.
For always giving me a helping hand,
And being patient enough to always understand.

For adding vivid colours to my black and white life,
Sometimes filling the holes of pain by making me feel alive.
For being a ray of sunshine on a pitch black night,
And for being the medium of warmth and love discarding the sorrow, everytime you hug me tight.

You complete my world Just like the stars in the sky, so bright.
Oh! How badly do we sometimes fight?
I love you and we are together a flawless couple,
You're the perfect piece of my life's puzzle.

19.A TEXT TO YOUR BOYFRIEND

With all my heart I write for you,
You're my sunshine on the day's blue.

With all my heart I write for you,
I wanna stick to you forever stronger than glue.

With all my heart I write only for you,
I can say countless times that I love you.

With all my heart I rewrite for you,
All those messages even when I'm angry upon you

With all my heart I say this to you,
I respect and value you and it's always true.

With all my heart I am writing this down,
I get sad with your every frown.

With all my heart you're always right,
Let's just shower more love and never fight♡

20.MUEZZA

He steps into the room and my heart gives a smile in his presence,
His tiny little paws leave footprints on my entire existence.

Softest fur all over the body, and those innocent little eyes,
His mesmerising meows and his presence makes everything nice.

Watching him eat, play and sleep he has become my permanent obsession,
He is the resemblance of my happiness and my most priceless possession!

That continuous wagging of tail and a mini nose that's fixed on his doll face,
Seen a hundred times or for the very first one, you will fall for him anyways.

My not so tiny pet fills my home with so much love and joy,
In this world full of countless creatures, he is my favourite boy!

EPILOGUE

•JAISE ISHQ ITNI AASANI SE HAASIL NAHI HOTA,
USEY HAASIL KARNA PADTA HAI!

KHWAAB BHI HAQEEQAT ME TABDEEL NAHI HOTE,
UNHE TABDEEL KARNA PADTA HAI!

•EVERY JOURNEY BEGINS AT SOME POINT, AND IT IS NEVER LATE TO BEGIN FROM WHERE WE LEFT IT OFF.

....

www.ingramcontent.com/pod-product-compliance
Lightning Source LLC
LaVergne TN
LVHW050341160826
845677LV00014B/3717